Where Do Ants Live?

Questions Kids Ask About Backyard Nature

Written by Neil Morris
Illustrated by Jan Lewis

READER'S DIGEST

Kids

Pleasantville, N.Y. • Montreal

Contents

Hi! How many times can you find us in this book?

I'm always last!

FINISH

Why do spiders make webs?

Spiders make webs to trap flies and other insects for food. The web is made of fine threads of silk, which spiders make inside their own bodies. The circular threads are sticky. When a fly gets caught in the trap, the waiting spider grabs it and eats it.

This is how a spider builds its web:

1. First, the spider spins a bridge thread.

2. Then it starts to add spokes in a Y-shape.

3. Then it adds more spokes and a frame.

4. It finishes with a spiral wheel of sticky silk.

4

To avoid getting caught in their own webs, spiders move along the dry silk spokes. Their oily bodies also keep them from sticking.

You can't catch me!

Still want to play spiders?

The ogre-face spider throws its web over the insect like a net and traps it.

The spitting spider squirts threads at the insect, sticking it to the ground.

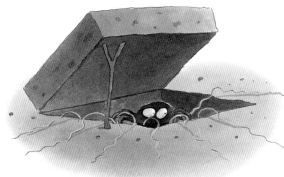

The trapdoor spider digs a burrow in the ground and leaves threads of silk outside. When a passing insect touches a thread, the spider jumps out and catches it.

What are clouds made of?

Clouds are made of billions of tiny droplets of water. They form when warm, damp air high in the sky cools down. There are different kinds of clouds. Each can give you a clue about what kind of weather is on the way.

Dark nimbostratus clouds bring rain.

When you see these patchy clouds, called cirrocumulus, it is a warning that the weather is going to change.

Water droplets in clouds bump into each other, making bigger and heavier drops. When they become too heavy to float in the sky, they fall to earth as rain.

Fluffy cumulus clouds usually mean there will be good weather.

A rainbow appears when sunlight shines through raindrops. The rain splits the light into seven different colors. Can you name them?

The colors of the rainbow are: red, orange, yellow, green, blue, indigo, violet.

Where does snow come from?

Like rain, snow comes from water in clouds. When it is very cold, clouds are cold, too. Then the drops of water in clouds freeze into tiny ice crystals, which bump into each other, making big snowflakes. The snowflakes float to the ground, covering the earth with a blanket of snow.

When you look at snowflakes close up, you see that they all have six sides. But no two snowflakes are exactly alike.

There is a lot of air in
snowflakes. That is what
makes them so light.

Phew!

It has to be very
cold for snow to
stay on the
ground. If it gets
warmer, the
snow turns back
to water and the
snowman melts.

Don't worry.
We can build
another one
the next time
it snows.

Where does the sun go at night?

The sun doesn't go anywhere. It never goes away, and it never stops shining. It gets dark at night because the earth turns away from the sun.

The earth is always turning. You can't feel it moving because you are moving with it. It takes a whole day for the earth to turn around once.

The earth is shaped like a ball. Only half of it can face the sun at a time, and on that half it is daytime.

The other half is dark because it is turned away from the sun. It's nighttime there.

Day in New York

When it is daytime for you, people on the other side of the world are fast asleep, because it is nighttime for them. What happens when you go to sleep?

Night in Tokyo

Night in New York

Right! When you're asleep, people on the other side of the world rise and shine! As your part of the world is turning away from the sun, theirs is turning toward the sun. So bedtime for you is morning for them.

Day in Tokyo

Why is it hot in summer and cold in winter?

Because of the way the earth travels around the sun — on a tilt. When your part of the world is tilted toward the sun, you have hot summer. When it's tilted away from the sun, you have cold winter.

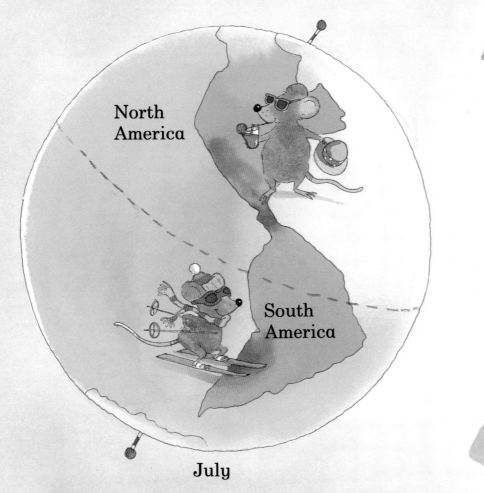

North America

South America

July

When the top of the world is tilted toward the sun, it gets the most direct sunlight. So it's hot summertime there. It's winter on the bottom half of the earth, which is tilted away from the sun.

Where does the moon go during the day?
The moon doesn't go away either. It's always there in the sky, but you usually don't see it during the day because sunlight is so bright.

A birthday riddle

Tom and Maria were both born on January 15. Tom's birthday is in the winter, but Maria's birthday is in the summer. How can this be?

Answer: Tom lives in North America, and Maria lives in South America.

As the earth moves around the sun, the seasons change. It takes a year for the earth to complete one orbit.

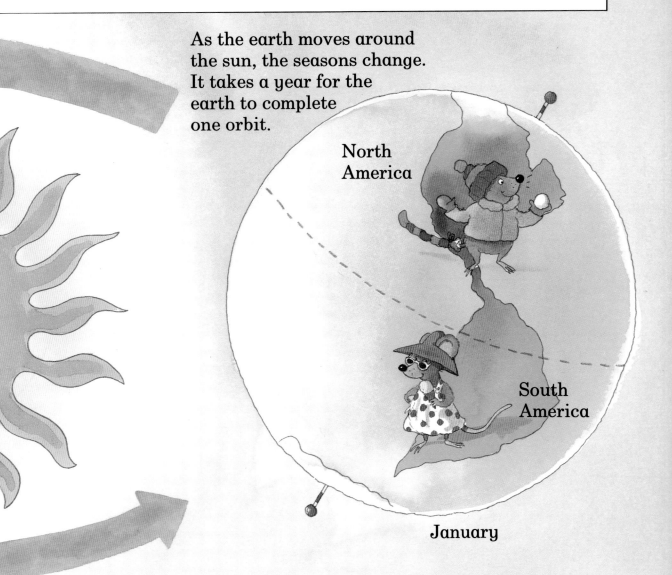

North America

South America

January

Now the top half of the world is tilted away from the sun. *Brrr!* It's cold winter. The bottom half of the earth now gets the most direct sunlight and has summer weather.

13

Why is grass green?

Because it has something green inside called chlorophyll. Chlorophyll has a job that's as big as its name. It helps grass and all green plants make their own food inside themselves. And no other living thing on earth can do that!

Sunlight

Each blade of grass is a food factory. It takes in water from its roots and a gas called carbon dioxide from the air. Then the sunlight turns that water and carbon dioxide into a sugary food that plants need.

Carbon dioxide

Roots

Water

The lines that you
see on a leaf are
called veins. They
carry the water
and food that the
plant uses to live
and grow.

Plants need sunlight to
make chlorophyll. If you
leave a bowl on a patch of
grass for a few days, the
grass turns yellow. It
can't make chlorophyll,
and without chlorophyll,
it can't make food. The
grass dies.

Why does thunder come after lightning?

Because lightning makes thunder. Lightning is a giant electric spark that you see as a big flash in the sky during a storm. The spark is hot, and it heats the air around it very quickly. This hot air crashes into cold air. The crash makes a loud boom — THUNDER!

BANG

BOOM

BANG

There's another reason why you see the flash before you hear the boom. Light moves much faster than sound.

The light of the lightning reaches your eyes before the sound of the thunder reaches your ears.

RUMBLE

RUMBLE

Thunder doesn't always sound the same. A deep, rumbling noise means that the lightning is far away. A loud crash means that it is nearby.

You can figure out how far away a thunderstorm is. Count the seconds between seeing the lightning and hearing the thunder. A gap of 5 seconds means the lightning is one mile away.

Why do some trees lose their leaves in the fall?

To save water. Trees get water from the ground through their roots, and they lose water through their leaves. In cold weather, trees can't get much water from the frozen ground. So if they didn't drop their leaves, they would dry out and die.

In the fall, the tree seals off the leaves' stems. Water can't get to the leaves, so the leaves die and fall to the ground.

Without water, leaves can't make green chlorophyll. As the green fades, you can see the bright colors that were there all along.

When spring comes, the buds on the branches burst open and new green leaves appear. They will make food for the tree until fall, when the leaves will fall once again.

In ice and snow, a tree looks bare,
But tiny buds are sleeping there.
What will the buds open up to be?
Just lift the flap and you will see!

Evergreen trees, which are always green, do not lose their leaves. Most have leaves shaped like needles, which don't give off much water. So evergreens can live through the cold winter without dropping their leaves.

By winter, the leaves have fallen and the tree may look dead. It's not! It's just resting until the warm weather returns.

Is there really a man in the moon?

No. Some people say they can see a face, but what they are actually seeing are dark and light patches on the moon's surface. With a little imagination, these patches look like a giant face gazing down on you!

How far away is the moon? The moon is about 239,000 miles from earth. Traveling that far would be like going all the way around the earth almost 10 times.

Moon walk
People used to think that some parts of the moon were full of water and called them "seas." But the astronauts found no water on the moon. It is dry and dusty — like a desert.

The moon has no light of its own. Light from the sun bounces off the moon and makes it appear to glow in the night sky.

Yuck! the moon's not really made of green cheese!

What's down in the ground?

There are many things that live under your feet! The roots of plants grow downward in the soil. Burrowing animals, such as moles, make their homes underground. And if you dig in the garden, you're sure to find wriggling worms and who knows what other treasures!

Rabbits dig burrows in the ground. A group of rabbit burrows connected by underground tunnels is called a warren.

Moles have clawed feet for tunneling through soil. They spend most of their lives underground.

Beneath the soil is rock. Deep down inside the earth, this rock gets so hot that it melts, becoming a hot, runny liquid. Right at the center of the earth is a solid ball of iron and nickel. So you couldn't dig to the center of the earth, even if you tried!

Why do birds sing?

Birds sing to send messages. It's their way of saying "Stay away from my nest!" or "Watch out — a cat!" Male birds sing love songs to attract females, and the females may answer with songs of their own. And sometimes, like you, birds sing just for the fun of it!

When a male bird finds a good spot for its home, it sings to tell others — "This place is MINE!"

The male sings a different song to attract a female. Then the two birds build a nest and raise their young.

Father cardinal

After me ... tweet, tweet, tweety-tweet!

Tweet! Tweet! Tweet!

Mother cardinal

A young bird learns its song from its father and then from other male birds in the neighborhood.

Birds call to warn each other of danger — perhaps a cat on the prowl. These calls warn birds of all kinds. No bird wants to hang around to become a cat's dinner!

Look out below!

Different kinds of birds have their own songs. The chickadee is named for its song. It tells you its name as it sings.

Chickadee-dee - dee!

Instead of singing, the woodpecker makes a drumming sound by pecking at a tree trunk. Male woodpeckers call to females in this way.

Why are flowers such pretty colors?

To attract bees! Bees look for flowers because they need the flowers' nectar to make honey. Little do the bees know that they help the flowers in return. By spreading the flowers' pollen, bees help flowers make seeds, which will grow into new flowers.

This pollen sticks to the bee as it flies away.

When a bee lands on a flower, some of the flower's pollen grains rub off on its body.

How does your garden grow?
Use the clues below to figure out what each seed will grow into. Lift the flap to see if you are right.

When the bee lands on another flower, the pollen rubs off onto this flower. The plant can now start to make seeds that will grow into new flowers.

These flower seeds are your first clue.
They will grow tall — taller than you!

These seeds have an important job —
To grow something yummy on the cob!

What is orange and often seen
At your door on Halloween?

Where do ants live?

Ants live in groups under the ground. Their homes have many rooms, joined by tunnels. The rooms are used for different things — to store food or garbage, to lay eggs, and to hatch baby ants. One special ant is called the queen. She is the mother of all the ants in the nest.

Work! Work! Work!

Some ants can carry fifty times their own weight. That's like a person lifting a car.

FOOD ROOM

BERRIES

SEEDS

FRUIT

INSECTS

The queen's jobs are to eat and to lay thousands of eggs.

EGG ROOM

GARBAGE ROOM

Dinner is served!

Ant eggs hatch into tiny white worms.

28

In summer, some ants hatch with wings. A few grow up to be queen ants, who fly away, dig nests, and raise new babies.

Oops!

EXIT

Most babies grow up to be worker ants for the nest. They find food, dig rooms and tunnels, feed the queen, and care for the babies.

The worms become cocoons in the nursery.

COCOON ROOM

I've come to take the next shift.

Thanks!

NURSERY

Ants are white when they hatch out of the cocoons. They soon turn black.

29

How does a caterpillar turn into a butterfly?

Just by growing up! It's hard to imagine, but that fuzzy bug with so many legs is actually the baby of a beautiful butterfly.

1. The mother butterfly lays her eggs on a leaf. When an egg hatches, out crawls a little caterpillar.

2. The first thing the caterpillar does is eat! It eats leaves all day, so it grows very quickly. Soon it's too big for its own skin! The skin splits, and the caterpillar wriggles out in a new skin. This happens four or five times as it grows.

4. One day, the bag splits and out crawls a soft, fragile butterfly. It spreads its wet wings out to dry. In an hour or two, the wings have grown stronger, and the beautiful butterfly can fly away.

3. When the caterpillar is full-grown, it weaves a bag around itself and hangs from a twig for several weeks. Inside the bag, wonderful things are happening. The caterpillar is turning into a butterfly!

A Reader's Digest Kids Book
Published by The Reader's Digest Association, Inc.
Produced by Larousse plc

Copyright © 1995, 1994 Larousse plc

Library of Congress Cataloging in Publication Data

Morris, Neil.
    Where do ants live? : questions kids ask about backyard nature / Neil
Morris ; illustrations by Jan Lewis. — Trade ed.
    p.   cm. — (Tell me why)
    ISBN 0-89577-607-3.
    1. Nature — Miscellanea — Juvenile literature. [1. Nature —
Miscellanea. 2. Questions and answers.] I. Lewis, Jan, ill.
II. Title. III. Series.
QL48.M863 1995
508 — dc20   94-14122
                                                       CIP
                                                       AC

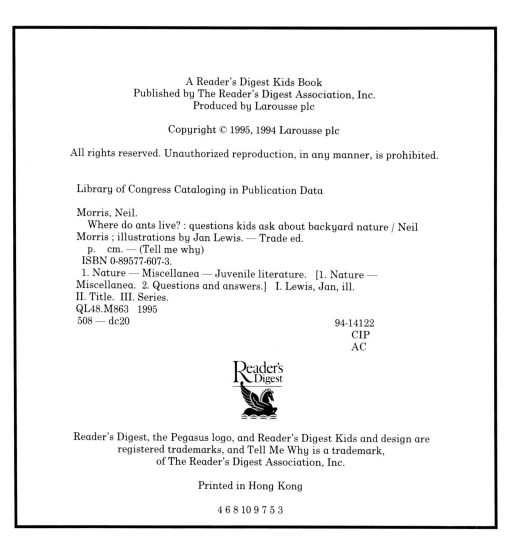

Printed in Hong Kong

4 6 8 10 9 7 5 3